To **Mom**

From **DAVE**

I Love You,

Other books in the TO-GIVE-AND-TO-KEEP™ series:
HAPPY ANNIVERSARY   To my very special HUSBAND
To a very special DAD   To my very special LOVE
To a very special DAUGHTER   To a very special FRIEND
To a very special SISTER   To a very special SON
To a very special GRANDMOTHER   To my very special WIFE
To a very special GRANDPA   Welcome to the NEW BABY
Wishing You HAPPINESS
To someone special IN TIMES OF TROUBLE
To a very special GRANDDAUGHTER

Published in 1992 by Helen Exley Giftbooks in Great Britain.
This edition published in 2008

12 11 10 9 8 7 6 5 4 3

ISBN 13: 978-1-84634-207-3

Illustrations by Juliette Clarke.
Written by Pam Brown. Edited by Helen Exley.
Important Copyright Notice: PAM BROWN © HELEN EXLEY 1992, 2008
Printed in China.
'TO A VERY SPECIAL'® IS A REGISTERED TRADE MARK OF HELEN EXLEY GIFTBOOKS

Dedicated: to Momtom

Helen Exley Giftbooks, 16 Chalk Hill, Watford, Herts WD19 4BG, UK.
www.helenexleygiftbooks.com

To a very special® MOTHER

Illustrations by Juliette Clarke.
Written by Pam Brown.
Edited by Helen Exley.

You took all the ordinary things
of every day and made me feel special.
Whatever happens in my life
I know, because of you,
that I am worth something.

HELEN EXLEY®

ONLY A MOTHER

Mothers know when you are faking.

Only a mother can send hugs by post.

Mothers can do running
repairs actually on the run.

Only a mother can make Family out of
an assortment of disparate individuals.

Only a mother can learn to see
through her children's eyes. If she
didn't, she wouldn't stand in a winter
drizzle, clutching a small, sticky paw,
staring at a workman down a hole.

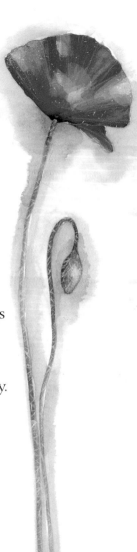

Mothers are the only people
who tell you the truth
when it's going to hurt.

Only mothers have lists.
That breed. And grow.

Mothers are the people who
yell after you waving the things
you've forgotten.

Mothers are always on stand-by.

THANK YOU!

Thank you for stocking me up with poems
and tunes to last me all my life.
Thank you for showing me the setting sun
for the first time.
And walking with me in the pouring rain.
And scrunching down winter beaches.
Thank you for letting me bring home
rocks and shells and fallen branches.
Thank you for housing my frogs.
Thank you for the
excitement of being alive.

Thank you for "Try hard. Work hard.
And if you can't do it,
turn your attention to something else."
Saved a lot of heartache.

Thank you for always being there.
Not intrusively. Not demandingly.
There.
Available at all hours for advice on coughs,
spelling, good books, stains, Mozart,
friends' presents, using libraries,
crossword clues. Et al.
Packed and ready to come if needed.
At once.
Shoulder to cry on.
Someone to tell the news.
Someone to laugh at the Funny.
Someone with an
inexhaustible supply of love.
Whatever I've done. Always.

A HAVEN

When I was very small and afraid,
you used to put on the light and show me
all the familiar objects in my room –
then flick it off and sit with me
in the darkness until
I was quite certain the shapes were constant.

Dad would insist you close the door
behind you, but you would always sneak
a crack of light into the gloom –
just enough to let me see that
nothing stalked my bed.

In a way it's still the same.
My anxieties are greater now,
and my world less certain – but you
let a little light into it, so that I can see
my problems for what they are.
Things I can deal with – not run from.

A mother is the person
who hears when you are grizzling
silently into your pillow.

When it's sorrow beyond keeping,
phone home.

Love is exciting.
But sometimes one needs
a quiet kitchen,
a cup of coffee and one's mother.

Mothers can dry your tears
down a telephone.

A mother has the magic glue
that sticks the
broken pieces together.

WORKING MOTHERS

Take in the laundry.

Collect the mended shoes.

Reading tests and driving tests and interviews.

Telephone and train times. P.T.A.

Cheese and crackers and pet rabbit hay.

Computers and portfolios,
manuscripts and mice.

E-mails and long-grained rice.

Measle spots and mergers,
the ballet school display.

And the television people are asking
for an interview today.

I am proud of what you do.

I love you for what you are.

I don't know how you fitted me in.
But you did.
And do.
Your life is so full – and yet I know that,
always, always,
There is room for me.

MEMORIES OF CHILDHOOD

I remember the run home from school,
black-stockinged, satchel swinging,
the drab day behind me, toast and currant
cake ahead. I remember the smell of home –
the smell all children hold in their noses,
the way puppy dogs do.

I remember you in the kitchen, apron wrapped
and waiting for my news.

And now here we are, one old lady
and the other one past the middle years,
sitting in a tea shop, our carrier bags
safely against our ankles, exchanging
the news of the week.

The years have changed us –
but brought us closer.
Mother and child – friends for life.

MOTHER LOVE

Mother love is more like tensile
steel than feathers.

Mother love is less meringue
than wholemeal loaf.

Mother love is the fuel that
enables a normal human being
to do the impossible.

Mother love doesn't need
as much sleep as other sorts.

Mother love doesn't care
what you look like. She thinks
you are beautiful, anyway.

Mother love is the most elastic
thing on earth – but even mother
love can be stretched too far.

Mother love does not come in a packet, like a Betty Crocker angel cake. It's a highly individual business – can sometimes sink a little in the middle and sometimes be rather crisp at the edges.

Mother love is the thing that makes a mother shake her child like a rat when he didn't get run over.

Mother love is like air. It's so commonplace you don't even notice it.
Till the supply is cut off.

Mother love is the family's pilot light.

WORRY! WORRY! WORRY!
Mothers live in perpetual terror – of fire
and flood and lonely roads, of evil men
and lunatic drivers, of failing brakes
and train derailments and aircraft
hitting trees. They only let it show about
three o'clock in the morning.

Mothers don't really have premonitions.
They have been over every possible eventuality
so often – both good and ill – that whatever
happens to you,
they've rehearsed it.

Hulking great muscle-bound heroes
whose mothers have access to their baggage
will find extra socks, vitamin C capsules,
snipped-out articles on the care
of the feet and packets of dental floss
tucked in among the pitons and ice axes.

Mothers are inclined to worry.
All the time.
Thanks, for not letting it show too much.

STANDING BY ME

I love it when you are excited and pleased
because I've had a success or a stroke of luck.
And I love it all the more
when you still think I'm wonderful
when I've fallen flat on my face.

Thanks for not coming over all weepy
when I've been unbelievably stupid.
Thanks for yelling and telling me what a fool
I've been. And then putting the raging
squarely behind us, and getting down to
sorting out what has to be done.

I know if I turned up on the doorstep
in the middle of the night, soaked through,
with all my bags and speechless with tears
you'd just say;
"Oh, love Take off all your clothes.
Put on my big woolly dressing gown."
Let's hope it will never come to that.
But it's nice to know.

Mother love is the conviction that all her geese
are swans. Which is the only way
to keep up the spirits of kids who are convinced
that they are lame ducks.

FOR EVERYTHING

Thank you for enduring the unendurable.
For making something out of nothing.
For giving when your pockets were empty.
For loving us when we were totally unlovable.
Thank you for doing the impossible
with a smile.
(Even if it quivered a little sometimes.)

Thank you for giving me your
complete attention when I explained
calculus to you.

Thank you for earning the money
to raise me. Thank you for meeting me
at the school gate.
Thank you for dealing with that Horrible Boy.
Thank you for putting raisins
in my lunch bag. Thank you for explaining
Taking Away and Multiplying.
Thank you for making mumps
not too bad at all.
Thank you for always being there when
I need you.
And for Surprises.

MOTHERS ACROSS THE WORLD

An engineer has a rapport with
the engineers of another country,
a mother with half its population.

Mothers know exactly what life is all about.
Not Art. Not Literature. Not Science.
All interesting stuff. Worth doing.
But basically, basically, it's about
children, about people.
You mothers should be the politicians.

Thank you for making friends with everybody
on a day out – ladies in art galleries,
bus drivers, shop assistants, old gentlemen
feeding the sparrows, old gentlemen
living in boxes, lost tourists, ladies on
the wrong bus....
Thank you for introducing us to
the human race.

Mums are an interlocking chain
that holds the world together.

FREE TO BE ME

From the very moment I was born, you insisted
that I was myself and not an extension
of you and Dad – that I had not come into
existence simply for you to organize or even
to love. Dear Parents – thank you for giving me
the freedom to love you.

Thank you for being interested –
but never prying. For being loving – but never
drowning me in love. For building me a nest
– but letting me fly free.

Thanks for opening all those doors for me –
but never shoving me through them.

Mothers start our lives. They cast on our
existence. They teach us plain and purl.
They give us the basic patterns.
But the good ones – the ones like you – hand
over the needles after a while, and say:
"There's the world, love. Choose yourself
some new shades, some new patterns.
Make yourself a life."

Good mothers give their children
paints and brushes and canvas,
but let them paint their own picture.

THANKS TO ALL MOTHERS..

...who made hard times seem good times.

...who faked their portions at dinner so that
everyone else got a little more.

...who said go ahead and finish it off –
they didn't fancy ice-cream.

...who persuaded us that living in a dirty
downtown area was exciting.

...who chopped up the best thing in their
wardrobe to make us a party frock overnight.

...who sang us home in the rain.

...who tried their hand at algebra.

...who shared our chickenpox.

...who managed to smile when we ran a fever just before they were due to go out for their birthday treat.

...who always found money from the tooth fairy – even if they had to hunt down the sides of the sofa.

...who only cried a very little when we broke the best teapot.

...who let us have our own opinions – just as long as we knew why.

...who let us grow up and fly free.